D1188456

What My
Golden Retriever
Taught Me about God

What My
Golden Retriever
Taught Me about God

RHONDA McRAE

P&R
PUBLISHING
P.O. BOX 817 • PHILLIPSBURG • NEW JERSEY 08865-0817

Printed in the United States of America

Library of Congress Cataloging-in-Publication Data

McRae, Rhonda, 1961-
  What my golden retriever taught me about God / by Rhonda McRae.
    p. cm.
  ISBN 978-1-59638-163-6 (hardback (printed case))
  1. Christian life--Presbyterian authors. 2. Dog owners--Religious life.
3. McRae, Rhonda, 1961- I. Title.
  BV4596.A54M38 2010
  231.7'2--dc22
                                        2010008072

Contents

Preface

I'M NOT CERTAIN, but I believe I can trace the genesis for this book back to a small group Bible study. I can't remember what book of the Bible we were studying or who the author of the lesson was. But I do remember that as we explored the various truths we were learning together, discussing the mysteries of God and all their implications for our lives, I discovered something about myself.

To me, the greatest of all the mysteries that God's Word proclaims is that God loves sinners. More specifically, that God loves me. In fact, although I don't remember a great many things about the Bible study, I remember remarking that if I could really understand that God truly loves me, Rhonda Louise McRae, my life would change.

Don't get me wrong. I grew up going to Sunday School and church. By God's great grace, I became a Christian when I was very young. I attended a Christian summer camp for years and even served as a counselor in my college days. I've heard all my life that God loves me. And frankly, it's always been more than I could take in and fully comprehend.

In fact, Jesus' proclamation to Nicodemus that "God so loved the world that He gave His only begotten Son" (John 3:16) has always been easier for me to grasp than his love for little old me. A huge, all-powerful God who can love millions and millions of people over the ages doesn't task my imagination. But to comprehend that He loves specific, weak, rebellious, sinful, proud, selfish me requires a leap that has always been farther than I had the ability to go.

Fortunately, God provided a living, breathing, inter-active sermon that has given me the clearest picture I've ever had regarding God's love for me. This Sermon has four legs, a cold black nose, an insatiable appetite for popcorn, and goes by the name of "Sadie." It is my sister's Golden Retriever who came to live with us as a puppy nine years ago.

It didn't take long for me to fall in love with the Sadester. Before long, my sister and I learned what made Sadie's tail wag. Early on, belly scratches were high on the list. So were chases. And the absolute best, best, best of all: the walk. It gives me such joy to know that there is something I can do to bring this level of pure bliss to Sadie. Her canine happiness when she knows she's about to go on a walk is worth whatever sacrifices I make to take her out the front door and onto the glorious, glorious sidewalk.

It was while walking Sadie one day that the question occurred to me, "I wonder if this is how God feels when He blesses me?"

Let me illustrate. Sadie can do absolutely nothing for me. She doesn't help pay the bills. She can't have supper on the table when I get home from work. She doesn't even do housework. In fact, she runs up the bills, has to be fed before I can consider taking a bite for myself, and makes a considerable mess in the house at times. Why, then, does it bring me such joy to give her joy? Why does she have the capacity to make me happy just by being herself? Simply because I love her.

When I considered the possibility that the same might be true in my relationship with God, many of the truths I've believed over the years started coming into focus in a new way. If I could love a dog, want what is best for her, and forgive her when she's been bad without ever ceasing to love her just as much, why couldn't God do the same for Rhonda?

That brings us to this book. Through my relationship with Sadie, I've come to see my relationship with God in a new way.

At this point, non-dog lovers may be rolling their eyes. But stay with me for a moment. Scripture makes it clear that God's creation helps explain who God is. Not fully, of course. We must carefully examine everything in the light of God's Word—His revelation—to know His character in the fullest way possible. But consider this:

> The heavens are telling of the glory of God;
> And their expanse is declaring the work of His hands.
> Day to day pours forth speech,
> And night to night reveals knowledge.
> (Psalm 19:1–2)

That which is known about God is evident within them; for God made it evident to them. For since the creation of the world His invisible attributes, His

eternal power and divine nature, have been clearly
seen, being understood through what has been made.
(Romans 1:19–20)

In light of this, is it surprising that God would
choose to teach me about Himself through a dog? God
the Creator chooses to reveal Himself—to show who
He is, what He is like—through what He has made.
In fact, His choice to teach me about Himself through
a dog manifests the specificity of His love for me. He
knew exactly how to reach me and did so lovingly.

There are two other points to consider about this
idea of learning something of God's character through a
Golden Retriever named Sadie. The first relates to one
of the sadder realities of the times in which we live.

That reality is the sad dissipation of families and
the resulting lack, in many cases, of the daily presence
of a loving, involved father within the family circle.
Whether through divorce, the absence of a marriage
covenant to begin with, or even the pseudo-separation
of workaholism, some dads are rarely if ever around to
enjoy, encourage, and discipline their kids.

How does a person whose experience with a father
has been so disappointing relate to the picture in Scripture

that God is our Heavenly Father? What can illustrate a tender, loving, involved, wise, wonderful, and authoritative Person to someone who has absolutely no frame of reference to understand that kind of relationship? To readers whose own father left a negative imprint, I encourage you to consider another illustration of Scripture: God as Master. True, the Master in Scripture is usually depicted in relationship to a servant instead of a dog, but there is value in considering God as Master in the context of Someone who has authority over us. And while Sadie might disagree at times, I generally have authority over her—which ties into my next point.

That is the concept that God—by the very nature of Who He is—has the absolute right to tell man what to do. However, though this never gets any press, everything He tells us to do, all His commands, are not only for His glory. They are for our good. Simply because He loves us. If that last phrase sounds familiar, it should. That's the lesson I've been learning from Sadie.

Finally, I am no trained theologian, so if you are hoping for brilliant arguments and complex insights, you might feel let down. I am a regular person who happens to be a dog lover, and by God's grace, a God lover. And because I've loved a dog, I've come to love her Creator even more.

CHAPTER ONE

Enter His Gates with Your Tail Wagging

SADIE IS THE QUEEN of the backyard. That is to say, while my sister and I are away at work, Sadie reigns over all she sees in the backyard. I'm usually the last one to leave in the morning. Before I go, I put Sadie's collar on her. Then, with Sadie almost jumping for joy, I lead her to the door with a huge bowl of popcorn in my hand. She hastens outside onto the patio and promptly sits and looks up expectantly at me.

Then comes the moment she's waited for. I throw a handful of popcorn over her head, then another to her right, and a third to her left. But she never even sees the second and third launches. She already has her head down, gobbling up the popcorn as fast as she can eat it. I tell her goodbye, then I'm off to work and Sadie starts her day outside. She never looks up.

But, boy, is it a different story at the end of the day! When the back door opens and Sadie sees I'm home, her attention is all on me. If you have a dog (and I'm guessing you probably do because you're reading this), you know what I'm talking about. What joy! What exuberance! What energy! What a greeting!

I'm not sure what your dog does, but when Sadie runs in the door when I get home—and I mean runs— her tail is up and wagging, her body unable to do anything but sprint at maximum speed. Around the couch! Stop! Bark! A quick check to see if I'm following. (I usually am.) Turn! Run the other direction! Bark! And the game usually ends with both of us panting and sitting together on a couch, happy to be together. It's pure canine joy, and I love it.

After one of these very happy welcomes from Sadie at the end of the day, I remember thinking if a Golden Retriever had written Psalm 100:4, it would have said something along the lines of "Enter His gates with your tails wagging!" She is the living, breathing, four-legged example of what it looks like to make an entrance expressing complete joy.

For more than a year, the idea of entering God's presence with my tail wagging didn't do more than make me smile, as I thought about how that kind of full-blown joy might gladden God's heart. And as a matter of fact, if that's all that can be gained from this comparison, that's still quite a lot. Oh, that I could give God the kind of pleasure that Sadie gives me when she goes completely off the charts with joy each time I come home!

But if I'm honest with myself, most of the time I don't enter God's presence with a Sadie-like natural exuberance. Most of the time, I enter with my head and my heart far away. Preoccupied. So although it doesn't come to me naturally as it does for Sadie, I think there's a lot to learn from her about the right way to approach God.

One thing that's obvious is that Sadie anticipates my presence. She knows what time I ordinarily arrive home from work each day, and you can bet she's close by the back door, listening and waiting. The minute she hears me inside or the light goes on, she's scratching on the door letting me know she's ready to come in!

Scripture is filled with passages telling of the writer's longing for God's presence.

As the deer pants for the water brooks,
So my soul pants for You, O God. (Psalm 42:1)

O God, you are my God,
   earnestly I seek you;
my soul thirsts for you,
   my body longs for you,
in a dry and weary land
   where there is no water. (Psalm 63:1, NIV)

At night my soul longs for You,
Indeed, my spirit within me seeks You diligently.
   (Isaiah 26:9)

Clearly, the saints of old experienced times when they felt deep yearning for fellowship with God. In many of those contexts, the longing for God was during a time of either spiritual dryness or of trial. What they had in common was their understanding that only in the presence of the One for whom they longed would they experience consolation and complete satisfaction within their souls. External factors might have created the longing, but they knew that only God could satisfy it.

I think that's one reason Sadie waits at the door for me. Her experience has taught her that when the door opens, her longing for fellowship (and let's face it, popcorn) will be satisfied. But only in the presence of the one who opens the door. The application here is pretty straightforward. I will anticipate God's presence more and move joyfully into His presence when I remember His goodness. When I recall that nothing satisfies the deepest longings of my heart like fellowship with Him. When I reflect that every truly good thing I have in life is from His loving hand.

But there's more to Sadie's joyful entrance than the careful watching and waiting. It's the no-holds-barred way she comes through the door without any sort of hesitation. She throws her entire self into it: barking, playing, running, tail-wagging, wagging, and wagging some more!

The opposite of what Sadie does is a very sad picture indeed. You've probably seen a dog—usually a stray—that has obviously been abused. Maybe he won't come near a human at all, or if he does, it's only with great hesitation and shyness. The abused pooch will slink up with its head tucked, and if you reach out to pet him, he might shrink back or even run away. That dog has learned not to trust.

But can we not trust God? Think, first of all, what it cost Him to make it possible for us to enter His presence. In John's Gospel, Jesus proclaims, "I am the door; if anyone enters through Me, he will be saved" (John 10:9). Jesus is the very door into the presence of God. And God opened that Door on Calvary when Jesus opened His flesh and shed His blood. In so doing, He took on Himself all the wrath we deserve for our sin, so we could have fellowship forever with God. Words can never express the cost of this sacrifice. Indeed, the price of admission into the presence of God is a cost so steep that we could have never paid it. God alone could purchase our way, and only at the expense of His own dear Son.

Secondly, think of God's invitation into His presence. The writer of Hebrews declares that we should "draw near with confidence to the throne of grace, so that we may receive mercy and find grace to help in time of need" (Hebrews 4:16). God Himself tells us

18

to come near Him through Christ with confidence. He has no more joy in seeing a slinking, cringing believer than I have in a dog that can't believe he's welcome. In fact, if my heart is touched by the sight of a cowering dog, imagine how the Good Master's heart yearns for a believer who, overwhelmed with guilt and shame, can't believe he is welcome.

Please don't take my word for this. Instead, listen to the encouragement from the Lord Jesus Himself in the Parable of the Prodigal Son. In the story, a much beloved son demands his inheritance, leaves home, throws away everything he has through wild living, and then falls into immense poverty. Finally, he comes to his senses and determines to return home. Though expecting nothing, he hopes to be brought on as a hired hand. Humbled as he is, he has no hope of welcome. And what happens? "But while he was still a long way off," Jesus says, "his father saw him and felt compassion for him, and ran and embraced him and kissed him" (Luke 15:20). Do you notice what the father did when he saw his long-gone son? He didn't wave to him and smile. He didn't walk to meet him. He didn't wait for his son to get to the front door. He ran to welcome his son home. To claim him as his own. To restore to him all the love and privilege he had ever known as a son.

Believer, never, ever doubt that you are welcome in the Good Master's presence. No matter what you've done; no matter what you haven't done, God has opened the door for you through Christ. If sin is keeping you away, it doesn't have to.

And why not enter His presence boldly? Scripture clearly states what awaits us there: mercy, grace, help. My tail is wagging already!

Maybe I'll never enter God's presence with the same kind of natural, joyful anticipation and confidence that Sadie shows when she comes through the back door each evening. But if I concentrate on just how good the Good Master is and what it cost Him for me to know Him, I'll definitely enter His presence with a more Sadie-esque spring in my step. A smile in my heart. A love and appreciation for my Master. I'll enter His gates with praise.

CHAPTER TWO

Under the Popcorn Bowl

HAVE I MENTIONED what a beautiful dog Sadie is? I know all dog owners think their dogs are beautiful, and they should feel this way. However, in my case, I think most people would agree with me that Sadie is gorgeous. She is from a line of registered Golden Retrievers that did very well in the dog show world, so she has many of the physical characteristics experts use to define the breed standard.

She also has the appetite of a rhinoceros.

I don't know if that's a breed standard or not, but the combination of her big appetite and her big bones has meant that Sadie is a hefty girl. Not tubby. Not huge. Not unattractive in any way. Just a little hefty.

My sister, being the good Boss Lady that she is, views this as a potential health hazard. After all, excess weight gets tough on a girl's joints as she ages, and none of us wants to ever see the Sadester struggle with arthritis and hip problems. So the question became, how do we help her slim up a little?

One of my sister's cohorts in the dog world suggested my sister try reducing the amount of Sadie's daily dog food and replacing it with some unsalted, oil-free popcorn, popped in the microwave. That kind of popcorn is low in calories, but still has a fair amount of fiber, so Sadie would still feel satisfied.

Well, to say that the popcorn was an immediate success is like saying Hurricane Katrina had some strong wind. Huge understatement. Sadie loves, loves, loves popcorn! To be honest, I'm not sure she tastes it, and I'm pretty sure she doesn't chew it. I think she just absorbs it.

The popcorn stays in the microwave popper—a funny, bowl-shaped container with a special liner in the bottom that somehow promotes the popping of the corn in the microwave. It's 2/3 cup for one minute and 38 seconds. I know this because popping corn is a routine business in our house.

After the popcorn has popped, it stays on the kitchen counter. Sadie can tell you that. One of her favorite spots in the house is on the cool tile of the kitchen floor, conveniently underneath the popcorn bowl.

Every time anyone gets up to go into the kitchen, Sadie goes, too. Whether you are a resident or a guest, Sadie is there to point out the popcorn bowl sitting on the counter, just in case you'd like to get her some. In fact, you don't really even have to be going to the kitchen for this attention from Sadie. You can be merely going through the kitchen to another destination inside or outside the house. The point is, as far as Sadie is concerned, you're getting close enough to the popcorn bowl that you might make it worth her while.

And by the way, just because you've given her corn one time doesn't mean that you can't give her more. If you have to make three trips to or through the kitchen, you can get her corn three times as well.

I realize I have belabored this a bit, but this characteristic of Sadie's has opened my eyes to what it looks like to live hopefully. And I think Scripture gives us a lot of reasons to live like that as believers. Let me explain.

When Sadie sees someone moving in the direction of the kitchen, she has all the reason in the world to believe her prospects of getting a few bites of popcorn are very good. Sadie expects someone will give her corn, because she has experienced it countless times before.

For believers who have experienced the outpouring of God's love and forgiveness through the cross of Jesus Christ, is the same not true? Can't we who have experienced the best of all possible blessings live hopefully before the Lord, trusting in His goodness and desire to bless us?

To me it seems that Scripture is painted throughout with passages encouraging us to live this way. Consider these examples.

"For I know the plans that I have for you," declares the Lord, "plans for welfare and not for calamity to give you a future and a hope." (Jeremiah 29:11)

For the Lord God is a sun and shield;
the Lord gives grace and glory;

No good thing does He withhold from those who
walk uprightly. (Psalm 84:11)

And we know that God causes all things to work together for good to those who love God, to those who
are called according to His purpose. (Romans 8:28)

Here are only three verses, but they are full of glorious
reasons to live with the expectation that God wants to
bless us. He says His plans are for welfare and to give
us hope; He promises that He doesn't hold back good;
and moreover, He will use everything that happens in
our lives in a good way. If that isn't a call for hopeful
living, I don't know what is.

Before we go on, it's important to realize I am not
dismissing the terrible sorrows and suffering that so many
Christians have experienced, both now and throughout
the course of history. Scripture makes it plain that all
believers will indeed go through periods of testing and
trial as part of their pilgrimage. Job has a lot to say about
that, and you could probably find a different story of
heartbreak on every pew of every church.

But the question I want to ask is this: Is it right
to expect that God's first and overall treatment of His

own dear children is such that would cause unrelenting despair? Should we assume this is God's first choice for us? Let me be even bolder. Do we, in fact, think less of God by not believing that He wants to pour out on us all the blessings that He can?

If I have a habit of routinely offering Sadie popcorn out of love and a desire to make her happy, why should I assume I am more likely to bless than God is?

Reflect with me on this passage.

> For if He causes grief,
> Then He will have compassion
> According to His abundant lovingkindness.
> For He does not afflict willingly
> Or grieve the sons of men.
> (Lamentations 3:32–33)

These verses make it clear that God does not take any pleasure in seeing the suffering of those He loves. The trials we must go through are out of His love and His desire to see us mature. But He is in no way untouched by our sorrow.

I think the best example of living hopefully and expectantly in light of God's goodness comes from the lips of the Lord Jesus in the Garden of Gethsemane. There, in the darkest of circumstances, Jesus prays in this way not once, but two times: "If it's possible, let this cup pass from Me."

The Lord Jesus certainly knew why He was in that garden. He was aware that everything in His life was leading to that point. But all of this knowledge never stopped Him from praying that the horrors of the cross be removed.

Is His example not enough to show us that our primary expectations should always be that God wants to do us good? And secondly, to trust that if suffering and sorrow should come our way, God has a reason for it and a way through it? After all, let's remember what followed the cross: total defeat of sin for all time, glorious resurrection and defeat of death, and exaltation to the right hand of God!

There's one final lesson I've learned from Sadie and the popcorn bowl, and that has to do with her practice of lying underneath the bowl. What she instinctively is doing is putting herself in a position where she is most likely to get popcorn. She might get popcorn in other places within the house (she has before), but 99 percent of the time she's near the popcorn bowl when she does.

27

Here's the point. Do I make a habit of putting myself in a place where I am most likely to receive God's blessings? Do I consciously make that choice?

One readily apparent example is the issue of worship on the Sabbath. People often say they don't have to be at church to pray or to fellowship with God. While this is perfectly true, it's funny how these individuals also insist that they can experience the blessing of God by appreciating His creation in the outdoors. Translation: golf course.

But God tells us in His word that He wants us to remember the Sabbath day to keep it holy, and that we shouldn't forsake our assembling together. Since this is clear from Scripture, doesn't it make sense that the popcorn bowl is more likely located in worship with His people than on the golf course, at the fishing hole, out jogging, or elsewhere?

That's just one example. But we know many other places where the popcorn is most likely to be, including:

- in fellowship with other believers
- in His service
- in prayer and personal devotions

Times of private prayer and reading of God's word offer some of the very plumpest kernels of blessing. Here, alone with the Good Master, we experience the most intimate fellowship. With no one else to hear or intrude, we can tell Him the very deepest longings of our hearts. We can seek Him without interruption and listen to His voice as He reveals His own heart in Scripture. There's truly nothing sweeter or more soul satisfying!

I think Sadie's got this one right on the money. If you want the popcorn, you've got to stay near the bowl. You've got to believe that popcorn can come at any time.

Do you think there's a popcorn bowl full of blessings for you? Do you believe God loves you and wants to give you what is good? I believe Scripture makes it clear that He does. Look expectantly to Him, trust Him, and see what blessings pop up!

CHAPTER THREE

The Leash of Liberty

IT WASN'T LONG AFTER I began thinking about my relationship with God through my relationship with Sadie that I considered the leash. It's hard not to think about a leash when it comes to Sadie, because it is a major source of emotion for the girl.

Sadie has a blue "flexi-leash" that we've used for her ever since she grew out of the puppy stage. Its lead is on some kind of tension roller, so when she walks way out in front of me the leash line expands to allow her to roam, but when she's walking closer to me it contracts to prevent slack.

When she was very young and it would come time for The Walk, Sadie would be so excited about the prospect of going out that she wouldn't sit still long enough for my sister or me to attach the leash to her collar. She'd run to the front door, spin around in circles, paw at us, and be so wiggly that there was no way to get the leash on her. And guess what? As long as the leash didn't make it to the collar, The Walk didn't happen. The longer Sadie fought the leash, the longer it took for her to get what she really, really wanted.

One day after I finally got the leash on Sadie and we were walking—Sadie out in front, tail high and happy in the air with a springy, joyful gait and nose sniff, sniff, sniffing everything—I thought to myself, "Sadie might fight the leash, but if she only knew—that leash is freedom!" It's the leash that allows her to go beyond the front door. Without it, she's restricted to the house and the backyard.

This idea that the leash equals not bondage but freedom helped me understand a phrase of Scripture I had never really grasped before. James, in discussing how true faith in Christ results in changed behavior, says this: "But one who looks intently at the perfect law, the law of liberty, and abides by it, not having become

32

a forgetful hearer but an effectual doer, this man will be blessed in what he does" (James 1:25). God's Word says the law is liberty. How is that possible? How is it that a set of do's and don'ts—restraints that essentially limit what I can and cannot do—is freeing?

And let's face it. We don't like restraints. We don't like anything or anybody having the ability to control what we do or don't do. Red light on the way to work? Grrr. Wait behind the line? Sighhhh. So the idea of law as liberty chafes.

Christians have a hard enough time dealing with God's commands. To the unbeliever, His commands are beyond ridiculous. Just last night on television, a soldier who had been deployed to rescue missionaries taken hostage mockingly wondered why these missionaries were setting up a church where no one wanted them. That TV show was a work of fiction, but it was an accurate illustration. As Christians, we're commanded to go into all the world to make disciples. To a non-believer, going to potentially dangerous foreign lands to reach people who don't have any apparent interest in what we have to say is nuts.

So how can any of us understand that the law equals liberty? Could it be that it is only through keeping

God's commands—wearing the leash, as it were—that we have the freedom to enjoy the very best God has for us? Notice how that verse in James ends: "this man will be blessed in what he does."

This is when I started considering why it's important to me that Sadie wear her leash when we're out for a walk. Maybe that would give me insight on why God is so interested in my keeping His commandments.

One parallel was obvious. I am fiercely protective of Sadie's safety. Even though we live in the suburbs and have nice sidewalks to use, there are still many dangers for a canine who is only interested in the joys that a walk holds for her. The first and most apparent danger is traffic. While we don't live on a busy highway, vehicles of all kinds are constantly going through our neighborhood as people go about their daily routines. Sadie has no fear of vehicles—or much else, for that matter. As far as she knows, the whole world exists to give her joy, and that big shiny thing with the black, spinning feet might have someone inside who would love her, right?

But what I know is that if Sadie were allowed to greet the big shiny thing in a way that made sense to her, the results could be catastrophic—even deadly. I must know that while we're walking, Sadie is by no means going to have a way to run out in front of a car. And if she isn't on a leash, I can't control that. So if she's not on a leash, no walking. See? The leash is liberty.

Because I love Sadie, I insist she wear the leash. Because God loves Rhonda, He insists I obey His commands. Both the leash and the law restrain us from doing whatever we please. But whatever we please may not be what is best for us. If you're still not convinced that God's law is truly the law of liberty, consider an encounter Sadie and I once had together with some other dogs in our neighborhood.

From time to time during our walks, Sadie and I have come across off-leash dogs. I know many people think as long as their dogs are in their own yard, it's perfectly fine for them to be off-leash. I'm sure that such pets are well cared for and loved; I imagine their owners simply think their dogs deserve a little roaming time. My guess is many of the owners let the dogs out on their own at certain times of day, probably to take care of business.

But one horrible incident with off-leash dogs stands out clearly in my mind. Sadie and I were enjoying a routine stroll one evening about nightfall. We passed a house on the far side of our neighborhood that is the home of three sweet dogs. Two of the three dogs are of a breed that loves to work and please their master. I'm convinced that the owners of these dogs believe their pets have achieved a level of discipline that would keep them from doing anything they shouldn't. But not on this night.

As Sadie and I went by their house, walking on the sidewalk across the street from them, two of the three off-leash dogs became still and alert. Slowly, they rose to their feet and started moving. Soon, they had crossed the street and come at Sadie and me, barking and staking their claim. In short order, the third dog, a much smaller, much yippier dog of another breed, came roaring over, too. As that little pup tore after Sadie and me, intent only on her objective of telling Sadie and me to get lost, she had no awareness of the SUV coming up the road. Sadie and I stopped. By this time the owner of the dogs had seen what was going on and was trying to call her dogs back. As the SUV got nearer and nearer that little dog, I stood helplessly by, screaming, realizing I was about to see that little guy get killed.

God was good to all of us, though, because the driver of the SUV saw the pup in time and slowed. The owner of the three dogs rounded them all up safely, and we went our separate ways. But I was angry and traumatized by what happened. Because Sadie was on her leash, I had the ability to control her during the fracas. But I had no ability to spare that other pup. All I could do was scream.

The point is, no matter how well disciplined, no matter how much the dogs may have loved their master and wanted to please her, they are still dogs. They still have a dog's instincts. They still need the leash. And Scripture says we are the same.

Consider Jeremiah's warning about man's nature: "The heart is more deceitful than all else and is desperately sick; who can understand it?" (Jeremiah 17:9). We may think we can know what pleases God without His commands; we might even want to please God in our own way, but the truth is that our own natures work against us. Our hearts deceive us. We need God's loving leash—His law of liberty—to keep us out of trouble.

Here's the thing. Just like that little pup, I'm not sure we always know where trouble is coming from. I could see that SUV coming, but the little dog couldn't. For one thing, the dog was completely absorbed in chasing Sadie and me, so he wasn't looking in the right direction. For another, because it was a very small dog, he didn't have the ability to see what I could with my far superior height.

But because God made us, knows everything about us, and sees our lives from beginning to end, He absolutely knows where danger exists for us. He knows how our instincts will betray us. And He's given us loving commands to protect us from harm. So the leash doesn't just equal liberty; it equals love.

In case you think all of this about the leash equaling liberty and love is still way off base, consider a final point.

I mentioned in the preface that God, by the very nature of Who He is, has the absolute right to tell man what to do. And He does. Even if He weren't loving, He still could demand our obedience to whatever commands He chooses, and enforce that obedience by whatever means He determined was most effective. But, oh, how far that is from God's loving heart! Scripture makes that clear in a number of places, but there's one that renders me speechless.

In Old Testament times, God made an astonishing statement Moses recorded in the book of Deuteronomy. "Oh that they had such a heart in them, that they would fear Me and keep all My commandments always, that it may be well with them and with their sons forever!" (Deuteronomy 5:29). The first time I read that verse, I was filled with wonder at what I saw, oddly enough, because of the punctuation. There's an exclamation mark at the end of this verse, denoting strong emotion. Emphasis.

And over what does God exclaim? He is moved with His desire that we keep His commands. And why is that? For His glory? Well, Scripture certainly teaches that all our lives should glorify our Creator. Is it for His reputation in the world? Again, Scripture is clear that God wants all people in all nations to honor Him and we are to promote that by lives that reflect obedience.

But what makes God exclaim here is something altogether different. He says, "That it may be well with them and with their sons forever!" God wants us to keep His commands because He knows they are good for us. He knows that as we keep his commands (obey the law of liberty), we are blessed in what we do. Wow!

Now that Sadie is an old hand at going for walks, she doesn't struggle as much when I'm trying to attach the leash. She's still excited to go and has to wiggle and jump and circle a little bit, but eventually she sits perfectly still while I hook the leash onto her collar. Even more, she only makes a move toward the door once I tell her, "OK, let's go!" Then, off we go to explore all the wonders the wide, wide world holds for a happy dog on a leash. Protected and restrained by the leash, she's free to enjoy the very best part of her day.

The "law of liberty"? You betcha! It's God's way of keeping me safe to enjoy all the blessings He has in store for me. And you, too.

CHAPTER FOUR

The Paw-Push Tail-Flick

I DELIGHT IN SADIE for a number of reasons. She's a beautiful dog, for one thing. Golden Retrievers have gorgeous coats with long reddish-blonde hair, white underbellies, floppy ears that need lots of fondling, and fluffy, happy tails. And Sadie is a gorgeous dog among a beautiful breed. She also has the happy, good-natured temperament that the breed is known for.

In addition to all the wonderful qualities of her breed, Sadie also has some charming little quirks that are uniquely hers. Some of them crack me up. One of them has taught me a wonderfully freeing lesson about God. I call it the paw-push tail-flick.

Sadie loves belly rubs. From the time she was a tiny puppy tearing around the house with that all-or-nothing energy that puppies run on, she has loved having her belly scratched and rubbed. In fact, as a puppy wearing my sister and me out with her jumping, scratching, biting, and other puppy craziness, the only thing that would stop her in her tracks was a belly rub!

Now as a grown girl, Sadie has invented her own way of asking for a belly rub. You guessed it. It's the paw-push tail-flick.

It goes like this. Imagine it's early in the morning. Picture my sister and me sitting in our den sipping coffee before getting ready to go to work. Sadie is in the den with us, stretched out near our feet, and one of us is rubbing her back with the toe of a house shoe. Slowly, Sadie rolls to her back, exposing her soft, white tummy. She makes eye contact with one of us, usually me, and then simultaneously pushes one paw toward me while giving her tail one or two little flicks. It's an unmistakable invitation to join her on the floor for the privilege of rubbing her belly. And it's irresistible!

I never get tired of seeing the paw-push tail-flick. It always charms me and makes me chuckle, and most of the time Sadie gets that belly rub that she wants.

I can't always stop what I am doing to give Sadie her heart's desire, but if I can, I usually do. She loves it, and I get pleasure from it, too. I like feeling her soft coat. I like giving her that joy. And I like sitting close by her side, enjoying her sweet nature.

In a dear and wonderful way, this funny little quirk of Sadie's has given me a new freedom in prayer. I've always easily understood that praise and thanksgiving to God are important in prayer. And of course that's true. If we ever grasped God's goodness and mercy toward us, they would inspire never-ending praise and thanksgiving. We wouldn't have time to do anything else. And it's always been easy for me to understand that God would welcome this kind of communication. After all, who doesn't like hearing "Thank you"?

Another important aspect of prayer is asking God for things. Scripture is clear that we should bring our requests before Him. But truthfully, deep inside I've wondered if that was equally welcomed before God. Aren't we taught to be content? To trust God in every circumstance in our lives, even when those circumstances are difficult? So how does all that fit in with asking God for change when we are not content and when our circumstances aren't easy?

That's where the paw-push tail-flick comes in.

If it's true that I never get tired of Sadie's unique little personal request for what makes her happy, could it also be true that I don't weary God with my requests? Could He, in fact, delight in the fact that I come to Him asking for the desires of my heart?

That, frankly, was a new idea to me. I think some of us by nature are better than others at asking for what we want or what we think we need. I've never been a very good asker. I wasn't good as an adolescent at asking my parents for money. As an adult, I'm generally not very good at asking for help, even when I really could use it.

I think some of this tendency has rubbed off over the years in my perspective on prayer. I've always known that Scripture teaches us to come to God with our requests, but I felt like a little kid going up to his harried, tired, cranky, overworked mother who was dealing with 10 million other kids, and tugging on the hem of her shirt for attention. Disruptive, to say the least. Maybe even unwelcome and annoying.

44

So Sadie's blissful freedom in coming to me for a belly rub any time she feels like it, which is quite often, was a new model for me. I don't find it irritating when she asks, even though it happens all the time. She doesn't irritate me because I love her and, as much as it is in my ability, I like giving her what makes her happy. Belly rubs, walks, popcorn—you name it. If she likes it, I give it.

Scripture has a lot to say about prayer as it relates to asking God for things. "You do not have because you do not ask," James tells us (James 4:2). Jesus Himself emphasized the importance of persistence in prayer when He told the parable of the widow who ceaselessly pursued a judge to seek legal protection, even though she knew he was most definitely not sympathetic. Luke explains that Jesus told that parable to "show that at all times they ought to pray and not to lose heart" (Luke 18:1). And, as Jesus pointed out in yet another passage in Luke, if men who are evil can be prevailed upon to do what we might ask, how much more will our Heavenly Father provide what we need (Luke 11:5–13)? So clearly, we are meant to ask.

There are a couple of other passages that don't relate directly to prayer, but that still resonate with what I am discovering about praying. These are more illustrative of the nature and character of the God Who hears our prayers. And they both deal with our expectations of God based on our understanding of Him.

First, the writer of Hebrews gives us this pearl of wisdom: "And without faith it is impossible to please Him, for he who comes to God must believe that He is and that He is a rewarder of those who seek Him" (Hebrews 11:6).

Notice what Scripture teaches that we must believe about God. We must believe that He is a rewarder. To reward someone is to give him something, and in the usual sense, a reward is a gift recognizing something good a person has done. According to this verse, God rewards a person for what? For seeking Him! And certainly one way we seek God is through prayer.

Most telling to me, however, is a parable the Lord Jesus told. In the very familiar Parable of the Talents recorded in Matthew 25, Jesus tells of three servants and their one master. About to depart on a journey, the master entrusted each of the three servants with the care of his estate while he was gone. The first two servants did their best with what they had been given, and when the master returned from his journey, he was very pleased with their efforts and rewarded them many times over.

The third servant is a different story. He made absolutely no effort on behalf of his master, giving this reason for his pitiful performance:

> Master, I knew you to be a hard man, reaping where you did not sow and gathering where you scattered no seed. And I was afraid, and went away and hid your talent in the ground; see, you have what is yours. (Matthew 25:24–25)

Interestingly enough, neither of the first two servants indicated any kind of fear or trepidation before the master. They worked hard and when the master returned he didn't hesitate to reward them richly. And Jesus said that they "entered into the joy" of the master.

Evidently, the master was fully capable of giving joy. Only the third servant, who perceived the master to be hard, selfish, and grasping, failed to experience it.

Could it be that the third servant had a wrong idea about his master that affected how he related to him? He didn't really think his master was a very nice person. And if we don't heed the instruction of Hebrews and internalize the idea that God is a rewarder, it will affect how we relate to God in many ways, but specifically in relation to prayer.

Think about it. What kind of boss is easier to ask for a raise? Boss #1, with whom you have a good relationship, who is always kind and supportive, and who has a history of generosity? Or Boss #2, who is quick to snap at you, shows very little appreciation for anything you do, and makes you feel inadequate in every way?

I fear that many of us make the same mistake the servant did. We think God is like Boss #2, when in actuality He is more wonderful than anything we could ever imagine Boss #1 to be!

So why is it so easy for Sadie to come to me so often? I think it's because she knows I will reward her. She trusts me. She knows I'm never going to hurt her, and she has experienced a lifetime of belly rubs, walks, and popcorn from me. When we trust God because we have a right understanding of what He is like, we will feel the freedom to ask Him about whatever is on our hearts.

But we can go even deeper. Remember how I described my delight in Sadie? Well, hang on to your seats. The Bible proclaims that God delights in us. Listen to the prophet Zephaniah's joyful assertion: "He will take great delight in you . . . he will rejoice over you with singing" (Zephaniah

3:17, NIV). Imagine! God singing about you! In fact, Scripture records God saying we are precious to Him! "You are precious in My sight, since you are honored and I love you" (Isaiah 43:4). If I don't get tired of Sadie asking for belly rubs—because I delight in her, because she's precious to me—can I in turn believe that I don't weary God by asking Him for things that matter to me?

I think it's informative at this point to see what Scripture teaches about what God doesn't like to hear. And trust me, it's the farthest thing from heartfelt prayer that anything could be.

Isaiah records this blistering comment: "Then the Lord said, '. . . this people draw near with their words and honor Me with their lip service, but they remove their hearts far from Me, and their reverence for Me consists of tradition learned by rote'" (Isaiah 29:13). Wow—isn't that clear? God seems fairly unimpressed with formulaic words that aren't connected in any way with what's really going on in our hearts.

There's one other thing to remember here. I don't give Sadie a belly rub every single time I get the paw-push tail-flick. Otherwise, I'd never get off the floor and go to work. Likewise, we know from experience that God doesn't give us everything we ask Him.

But here's the absolute truth about the way God answers our prayers. He always, without fail, gives us what is the very best for us. Jesus made that clear.

> Or what man is there among you who, when his son asks for a loaf, will give him a stone? Or if he asks for a fish, he will not give him a snake, will he? If you then, being evil, know how to give good gifts to your children, how much more will your Father who is in heaven give what is good to those who ask Him! (Matthew 7:9-11)

We, of course, have limited understanding of what is good for us. We may think we're asking for a piece of bread and what we really are asking for is a snake. Out of love, God will instead give us bread.

Why can we imitate Sadie in her blissful paw-push tail-flicking? Because God finds us precious. Because He wants to give us bread, not a snake. And ultimately, when we come to God trusting in His goodness, no matter how He chooses to answer our prayers, we are showing that we have a right understanding of Who He is.

And now, if you'll excuse me, I think I'll go give Sadie a belly rub.

CHAPTER FIVE

Socks and Closed Doors

SADIE IS NOT an outside dog. She is an inside, outside, inside, outside, inside . . . well, you get the picture. She comes and goes as she pleases, restricted only by how often she can get a human roommate to open the door to the backyard for her.

Truthfully, the point of allowing Sadie to come inside the house is for fellowship. We live in the Deep South, and brother, does it get hot here. We knew before we got Sadie that if we were ever going to spend time with her, she would have to come into the house.

Going outside to fellowship with a dog in 90-plus-degree heat and 90-plus-percent humidity was never a strong likelihood. So Sadie comes inside to play with us, and we are all happier.

Within the house, Sadie is allowed on the furniture. I know many of you who have much nicer homes and furnishings than my sister and I do must be horrified. True, an inside dog is hard on housekeeping. But I don't regret a minute of it. What she lacks in cleanliness she more than compensates for in love.

Among the various pieces of furniture and flooring choices, Sadie shows an amazing lack of discrimination. She'll crawl up on anything or lie low on any surface. Just the other day while I was working on this book, I passed through the den several times in between writing and doing laundry. First Sadie was on the floral sofa. Next she chose the burgundy recliner. Then the white sofa. The cool wooden floor. The white wingback. The marble hearth. I think she sampled every possible surface the den offered for her comfort and taste.

You see how it is. Within our house, Sadie has enormous freedom. Freedom to go out and come back in. Freedom to select her own comfy spot. There's only one place that is more or less routinely off limits to

Sadie. And sadly, that's her Boss Lady's bedroom. It's because Sadie is a sockaholic. And the door to that room stays closed almost all the time.

As a puppy, Sadie acted like most puppies. Once she got a sock, a dishrag, a towel, a shoe, or anything else she could get in her mouth, the chase was on. She would take off running, slobbering all over whatever item she had in her mouth at the moment, and it was up to my sister and me to catch her, remove the doggy-moistened object, and try to teach her not to do that. Mostly, it was a losing game. Our only hope was to come at her from different directions and trap her between us. Whenever Sadie would see that happening, she'd run and hide behind the white chair, with her mouth underneath it. One of us would drag her out, pry her mouth open and remove the yuck-o, slimed up item that she had tried to claim as her own.

I'm thankful that Sadie has outgrown most of this. She is for the most part a sweet, mild-mannered, happy lady. But to this day, she will not resist a sock. She loves them. She seeks them out. When she finds one, she slips off quietly to chew and chew and chew in private. And when she is discovered by my sister or me, she goes back into puppy mode and tries to hide behind the same white chair. This tells us that she knows she is misbehaving, but she doesn't seem to care.

Unfortunately for Sadie, my sister has an occupation that requires her to work in tennis shoes and socks every single day. So a ready supply of clean, non-holey, matching socks is a daily requirement for the Boss Lady. The supply room for socks is my sister's bedroom. My sister needs them; Sadie covets them. My sister is Boss, so the door to the bedroom stays closed until it's time for bed, and they go in there together, my sister to her bed, and Sadie to her kennel.

I've made light of the whole sock situation, but at times it's really not funny. As I mentioned before, my sister really needs socks and because she's on her feet a lot at work, she doesn't buy cheap socks. She has been very frustrated at times to come upon Sadie unaware, completely destroying a brand new pair of work socks.

I think that in a very small way, this is a picture of the way sin affects Christians. If you are an unbeliever reading this book, this analogy doesn't really work for you. In your canine comparison, you have not yet become a resident in a home where you are cared for and loved. And your problems are a lot bigger than socks.

But for Christians, there's something to think about here.

What are your socks? What things in your life do you know God would have you leave alone, but you persist in seeking them out regardless? Every Christian struggles with sin. Scripture confirms this in 1 John, where the beloved disciple of Christ flatly says, "If we say that we have no sin, we are deceiving ourselves and the truth is not in us" (1 John 1:8).

We all have our personalized, individual socks—areas of temptation that never seem to go away. But how do these socks affect us? The Boss Lady doesn't ignore socks, and God does not ignore sin. You don't have to look any farther than the cross to see how serious sin is to God. What it cost God to deal with our sin is nothing less than His Son.

When Sadie is caught red-pawed with a sock, she definitely loses the sock. She loses the praise of the Boss Lady. But she never loses her permanent place of love and security in this house. She still enjoys many of the same privileges to come in and go out as she pleases. And, most of all, she never loses the love of the Boss Lady or me.

How wonderful it is to know that in much the same way, God doesn't kick us out of His family when we sin! He still loves us just as much. He doesn't stay mad at us all the time. But don't take my word for it. Hear it from the Word of God.

> For I am convinced that neither death, nor life, nor angels, nor principalities, nor things present, nor things to come, nor powers, nor height, nor depth, nor any other created thing, will be able to separate us from the love of God, which is in Christ Jesus our Lord. (Romans 8:38–39)

Let's not stop with Paul. What does the Lord Jesus have to say about this?

> My sheep hear My voice, and I know them, and they follow Me; and I give eternal life to them, and they will never perish; and no one will snatch them out of My hand. (John 10:27–28)

The forgiveness that Jesus won for us on the cross is for all time. Our position in God's family is forever.

Our place in His heart is there for eternity. But the truth is, sin does have consequences. And I can't help but wonder if the closed door that Sadie earns when she sneaks off with a sock is a fairly good illustration of what sin costs us.

What is a closed door except a barrier? A door is a place where division occurs. It ends the communication between people (and dogs) in two different rooms. And in a similar way, our sin creates barriers between us and the full enjoyment of all God wants for us.

What doors do our socks close? As in Sadie's case, sin closes the door to freedom. Scripture teaches that sin leads to slavery. Jesus says, "Truly, truly, I say to you, everyone who commits sin is the slave of sin" (John 8:34). And Peter, warning early Christians to stay away from false teachers who were corrupt, issues this sobering statement: "For whatever overcomes a person, to that he is enslaved" (2 Peter 2:19, ESV). Do you see what happens? We become controlled by the sin that we refuse to control.

But the worst thing about sin is that it puts a barrier between God and us. The rich fellowship we can experience with God is diminished when we refuse to forgo our socks. The Psalmist says, "If

I regard wickedness in my heart, the Lord will not hear" (Psalm 66:18). And John, in reminding us that God is light in Whom there is no darkness, puts it very bluntly. "If we say that we have fellowship with Him and yet walk in the darkness, we lie and do not practice the truth" (1 John 1:6).

While my sister and I may not always know the best way to help Sadie conquer her addiction to socks, God is a perfect, loving and wise Master in every way. He loves us and He longs for us. And because of His great love and longing for us, He will deal with us perfectly about any socks we may be harboring.

The writer of Hebrews assures us that "those whom the Lord loves He disciplines" (Hebrews 12:6). God knows exactly what each of us needs to help leave the socks behind. He deals with us in the same way that he instructs the wise farmer to tend each kind of crop that he raises, as recorded by the prophet Isaiah.

> Does the farmer plow continually to plant seed?
> Does he continually turn and harrow the ground?
> Does he not level its surface
> And sow dill and scatter cummin
> And plant wheat in rows,

Barley in its place, and rye within its area?
For his God instructs and teaches him properly.
For dill is not threshed with a threshing sledge,
Nor is the cartwheel driven over cummin;
But dill is beaten out with a rod, and cummin
      with a club.
Grain for bread is crushed,
Indeed, he does not continue to thresh it forever.
Because the wheel of his cart and his horses
      eventually damage it,
He does not thresh it longer. (Isaiah 28:24–28)

Don't miss the picture. Just as He taught the wise farmer, God knows that what would break some wouldn't harm others. God's discipline is always what is best for us. And He never mistakes what His children need. Our friend, the writer of Hebrews, gives us this final word of encouragement: "All discipline for the moment seems not to be joyful, but sorrowful; yet to those who have been trained by it, afterwards it yields the peaceful fruit of righteousness" (Hebrews 12:11). His discipline is to train us to walk in the joy of fellowship with Him.

The Boss Lady and I have had very limited success in determining an appropriate punishment to keep

Sadie away from socks. But God does not experience any limitations in His wisdom and understanding of what's best to do with His sock-chewers. Any discipline He may send to His beloved children is always suitable, always perfect, and always sent from a heart overflowing with love.

One final thought about socks and sin. The real nature of sin is deceit. When Sadie bites down on that tasty sock, she is lost in the moment and nothing matters but that sock. She doesn't realize that what the sock really means is scolding and closed doors and loss of time with the Boss Lady.

The same is true of sin. It deceives us. We think that sock—whatever it is—is going to give us something we desperately want. But the truth is, sin can never, ever deliver on its promises to us. That's because every sin has its root in a big lie from the pit of Hell.

This is important to understand. Jesus described Satan, the one who encourages us to keep looking for socks, in this way: "He was a murderer from the beginning, and does not stand in the truth because there is no truth in him. Whenever he speaks a lie, he speaks from his own nature, for he is a liar and the father of lies" (John 8:44). When you buy what he's selling, you've been tricked.

60

Sin deceives us and then closes the door between us and the One who loves us more than we have the ability to comprehend, exactly as Adam and Eve discovered. One bite of the forbidden fruit and the door closed between them and face-to-face fellowship with God in the perfect garden He created.

Before we leave this examination of what Sadie has taught me through socks, I want to go back to the passages in 1 John that we touched on in the beginning. As we discovered, we all struggle with sin. John pointed out that we are deceiving ourselves when we say that we don't.

But what John says immediately following that inescapable reality holds the key that will open the doors we've closed. "If we confess our sins, He is faithful and righteous to forgive us our sins and to cleanse us from all unrighteousness" (1 John 1:9). God has promised to forgive what we confess. No matter how filthy our particular socks may be, God's forgiveness is waiting to wash them clean.

When I first contemplated this concept of socks and closed doors, I was comforted by getting a sense of how God could still love me just as much when I sin against Him. After all, I still love Sadie just as

61

much even when she is being very bad. God's love in this way fills me with wonder and thanks.

But the other truth makes me ponder as well. Are there blessings waiting behind a door that will remain closed until I can be trusted to leave the socks alone? I don't know about you, but I'm praying for grace to obey and find out.

CHAPTER SIX

Right by My Side

WITH ALL THIS TALK about Sadie—her beauty, her happy and affectionate nature, her love of popcorn—I think it's possible that I have failed to communicate the existence of a trait that might seem uncharacteristic. In spite of her great love for all people everywhere, particularly her Boss Lady, Sadie is also Miss Independent.

If you're on the couch, she might want to get up there, too, but on her end, thank you very much. Or if, perchance, she should choose to recline on the cool, cool tile of the marble hearth, she doesn't really need you there with her putting kisses on her nose. And if my sister and I want to enjoy a television show in the den, fine, but she'll just stay in the kitchen near the popcorn bowl. Loving, you see, but not a cuddler. Needs and likes her own space.

My sister and I always enjoy Sadie's companionship, and when she's in the kitchen while we're in another room, we'd love for her to join us. But we don't force it. It's just another of Sadie's own little ways.

So loving the Sadie girl like I do, imagine how it delights me on those all-too-rare occasions when she comes and just sits by my side. Sometimes I'll be reading the paper. Or maybe I'm having morning devotions when she walks up and lies at my feet. It's so sweet. It makes me want to drop everything and give her a belly rub and return that affection!

This is completely different from the attention I get from Sadie most of the time. Ordinarily, I have her attention when she wants something from me. Nine out of ten times it's popcorn. Or maybe she needs to go outside. Or maybe she needs to play. Or a belly rub.

The point is that she rarely comes to sit with me or be with me just because it's me. Nearly always, she's seeking something from me.

Sadly, I think this is the attention I give God most of the time, too. Having a hard day? Lord, give me strength. Going shopping? Lord, how about a good parking place! Finances feeling strained? Lord, please let me get an income tax refund. Me, me, me. I need. I need. I want. I want.

But how often do I enter His presence just because I love Him? Just because of how wonderful He is? Just because I want to gaze at Him? Just because I want to be with Him?

I think, in a very small way, this may be the true meaning of worship. When, as Sadie does on occasion, I just go and sit by His side not asking anything, not demanding anything, but just being with Him for His sake alone.

Maybe, like Sadie, it's not our natural inclination to do this. I confess I am naturally all too self-absorbed. And I see how this tendency flavors my personal devotions and times at church. Instead of thinking of God, being in His presence, and fellowshipping with Him, I'm making out my spiritual grocery list of all the things I need to manage my life in the way I think it should go.

But I wonder if an amazing thing happens when we worship God for Whom He is apart from what He gives us. Think about this passage from James in a new way: "Draw near to God and He will draw near to you" (James 4:8).

I don't ordinarily imagine things in high definition, but I have pictured in my mind how this verse might look if we could see it. I imagine the throne room of Heaven where God Most High, ruler of all that was, is, and ever will be, reigns in absolute sovereignty. Suddenly, in the midst of all the glorious activities of Heaven, the Lord stops and gazes downward, focusing completely on a beloved saint who is truly lost in love and worship of God alone. Not thinking of himself. Not dwelling on her needs. Not distracted by doubts and fears. But only thinking of and gladdened by the thought of Who God is. And in that moment, God draws near to that saint in fellowship of the sweetest, closest, and most loving kind.

Could it be that because of God's great love for us, when we stop asking and start loving Him for Who He is, He finds us irresistible? In her own way, Sadie has taught me how this might be. When she comes and just sits by my side, my heart melts. No matter what

I'm in the middle of doing, I have to respond to her somehow—a scratch on the head, a little rub on the side of her cheek, or a full-blown belly rub. Something.

There's so much about this that I realize I don't know yet. Experientially, I understand very little when it comes to the true worship of God. Even Sadie, popcorn hound that she is, still knows a little something of loving me without asking for anything in return. I still have a lot to learn from Sadie about this kind of selfless, God-focused love and worship. But it fills me with joy knowing that the work of my life may be in learning how to worship, and that the glory of Heaven will be worship without end.

Rescue

I LOVE TO SEE SADIE comfy and happy. I get a lot of pleasure watching her rolled into a doggie curl, her chin resting on one or both of her front paws, enjoying a good nap. I especially love it when I can tell she's having an exciting dream. She makes funny little squeaks, her legs twitch, her mouth quivers. Obviously, there's something wonderful going on in Sadie's dream world. It's the good life, and there's no mistake about it!

But in this last little reflection about what I've learned about God through my relationship with Sadie, I have to recount a story that's far removed from a dog enjoying the good life.

Earlier this year I watched the movie *Eight Below* with some good friends. It's based on a true story of sled dogs left behind in Antarctica when the scientific team they were stationed with was forced to evacuate ahead of a terrible storm. The dogs were alone all winter, facing the worst of cold, snow, and icy conditions with no food or help of any sort.

I love watching movies, and this was certainly a clean family film. But it about killed me to watch. In fact, I watched most of it—except the very beginning and the very end—between my fingers!

Loving dogs the way I do, it was hard to watch the terrible deprivation those dogs endured. They had to struggle to survive. They were under attack from the climate and predators. Their lives were relentlessly hard and dangerous.

As I watched the movie, I couldn't help but think how glad I was that Sadie was safe at home, napping comfortably in her kennel. She had enjoyed a nice supper with plenty of popcorn, and she was protected as she could be, with a nice roof over her head. Plus, we would be home soon to give her lots of love and companionship.

But I hated the fact that the real-life animals portrayed in the movie had suffered so much. And because

God had been teaching me so much about Himself through Sadie, I tried to think about those tremendous dogs in light of all I had been learning. If I had been miserable just watching a movie about abandoned dogs, how must God feel to see so much of humanity suffering day in and day out? With His heart of love, how can God stand it?

And then it hit me. He couldn't.

As I write this, fittingly enough it's two days before Christmas. My family will celebrate in traditional ways. We'll open gifts Christmas morning. My mother will have a lovely turkey with dressing and all the Southern fixings. We'll eat too much, watch a fair amount of football, and be glad we are together as a family to share love and make memories. And unless I am careful, I'll fall into the trap of forgetting what it's all really about. It's a rescue.

On Christmas, God launched a rescue operation that changed the course of history. He couldn't stand to see mankind suffering the deprivation that sin brings. He could not tolerate the broken lives, hopeless longing, and struggle for meaning that we experience when we are without Him. So, He came. He came Himself to rescue us from an existence that is far more dangerous and relentlessly harder than those dogs knew in the barren winterscape of Antarctica.

At the nub of everything God has shown me about Himself this year through Sadie is the glorious reality that the Good Master's heart is overflowing with love. It's a love that left Heaven to come into the world to rescue hurting, lost, sinful mankind.

To rescue sinful me.

In the movie, after the dogs were left behind, they adapted, learned to find food, and could cope with the terrible conditions they were forced to endure. But it was far from the safety and comfort they had known while their master was with them. And they were without the companionship of their master, too.

In the same way, I can't help but wonder if those who don't know the Good Master truly know peace. Do they know what it's like to have absolute confidence no matter what life holds? Do they understand how it feels to know Someone is protecting them and loving them every minute of every day? Someone who will finally welcome them into His own presence where there is "fullness of joy"?

Jesus said, "I am come that they might have life, and that they might have it more abundantly" (John

10:10, KJV). All the Good Master has for us is not just for Heaven. It's for right now, right where we are. In *Eight Below*, the presence of their master made all the difference to those dogs. And it's the same with us. We need our Good Master. We need Him now and forever.

There's at least one big difference between the master in the movie and our Good Master. But it's a very important difference. A terrible storm separated the master in the movie from his dogs. But there is nothing in Heaven, Hell, or Earth that can separate the Good Master from those who belong to Him. He promised that He would never leave us nor forsake us.

Right now, Sadie is sleeping soundly in her kennel. Her Boss Lady is enjoying a nice pre-Christmas nap as well. All is calm, all is bright in Sadie's world. As for me, I am resting soundly in my Savior. Out of His great goodness, He has used a sweet, beautiful Golden Retriever to show me His own tender heart of love. Through this journey, I have learned to trust Him more than ever. He has quickened my hope for the days ahead. Truly, my Master's pleasure is more and more my own. And being in His presence is the best place of all.

73

If you don't know the Good Master, please open your mind to the possibility that you need to be rescued. You were meant to enjoy a relationship that is everything your heart longs for, even if you don't know exactly what that might be. Call on Him through the Lord Jesus. Seek Him as He offers Himself through the gospel. He has promised to be found by all who seek Him. You will be rescued. Saved.

If you already know the Good Master, I hope that you will see, as He has shown me, that His love for you is greater than anything you could have ever hoped for or imagined. Trust Him and follow Him. Mind the leash. Leave the socks alone. Look for the popcorn. And stay right by His side.

Dog Biscuits
Extra Treats for Study and Reflection

Chapter 1: Enter His Gates with Your Tail Wagging

WHAT I LEARNED ABOUT JOY

"She is the living, breathing, four-legged example of what it looks like to make an entrance expressing complete joy."

Because Jesus Christ made the way for us to enter God's presence, there are many reasons we can enter God's presence with unrestrained, full joy. Do you feel free to relate to Him without fear and guilt? What have you learned about joyfulness before the Lord?

Chapter 1: Enter His Gates with Your Tail Wagging

Chapter 2: Under the Popcorn Bowl

WHAT I LEARNED ABOUT HOPE

"Sadie expects someone will give her corn, because she has experienced it countless times before."

To bring us into a relationship with Himself, God didn't spare His own Son. What does this show us about His mindset toward us? What have you learned about living hopefully in light of God's character and actions?

Chapter 3: The Leash of Liberty

WHAT I LEARNED ABOUT TRUST

"How is it that a set of do's and don'ts—restraints that essentially limit what I can and cannot do—is freeing?"

God's love and protection of us through His Word and through His sovereign direction in our lives might not always be easy to see or understand. Does it help to remember that He knows and sees so much more than we have the ability to know? What have you learned about obedience and trust?

CHAPTER 3: THE LEASH OF LIBERTY

Chapter 4: The Paw-Push Tail-Flick

WHAT I LEARNED ABOUT PRAYER

"If it's true that I never get tired of Sadie's unique little personal request for what makes her happy, could it also be true that I don't weary God with my requests?"

Scripture gives us countless invitations to bring our requests to God in prayer. But do we secretly wonder if we get on God's nerves? Can we instead remember that He delights in us? What have you learned about prayer, and especially freedom in prayer?

Chapter 5: Socks and Closed Doors

What I Learned About Forgiveness

"But she never loses her permanent place of love and security in this house."

Sin is something that will affect believers as long as we live. But it can never undo the once-and-forever security we have through Jesus Christ. But do we really believe this wondrous truth, or do we somehow feel that God holds grudges? What have you learned about forgiveness and the consequences of sin?

Chapter 6: Right by My Side

What I Learned About Worship

"So loving the Sadie girl like I do, imagine how it delights me on those all-too-rare occasions when she comes and just sits by my side."

Have you ever considered what God must feel when you enter His presence just because you are glad to be with Him? Have you ever thought about worship as a way of bringing pleasure to God? What have you learned about worship?

Chapter 6: Right by My Side

Chapter 7: Rescue

What I Learned About Real Life

"He could not tolerate the broken lives, hopeless longing, and struggle for meaning that we experience when we are without Him. So, He came."

God's heart is moved with compassion for sinners. He didn't stop at the pain and humiliation of the cross to save us from the deadliness of sin and life without Him. His love moved Him to action. What have you learned about where real life can be found? Do you need to be rescued? Do you know others who need to be rescued?

Chapter 7: Rescue

Rhonda McRae has a degree in communications from Mississippi University for Women and works as a creative writer and editor at Baptist Health Systems, one of Mississippi's largest healthcare organizations. She is a member of First Presbyterian Church of Jackson, Mississippi, where she sings in the choir and also teaches the "New Twos" Sunday school class.

Rhonda and her sister Gina live with Sadie, the golden retriever, and Lanny, the yellow Labrador retriever, near Jackson, Mississippi. Sadie has taught Lanny the joys of popcorn, and now he wants his own book.